BIG TRUTH LITTLE BOOKS®

God Defines and Defends Marriage

Cliff McManis

GBF Press
Sunnyvale, CA

God Defines and Defends Marriage is volume 7 in the **BIG TRUTH little books**® series

---

General Editor
Cliff McManis

Series Editor
Derek Brown

Associate Editors
Breanna McManis
J. R. Cuevas
Matt Yrizarry

Published by GBF Press. Find us online at GBFPress.com

Requests for information about **GBF Press**® can be sent to:

GBFPress@gbfsv.org

ISBN-13:978-0692872284
ISBN-10:0692872280

Cover Design: Josh Guglielmo
Proofreader: Jasmine Patton

Marriage is to be held in honor among all, and the marriage bed is to be undefiled; for fornicators and adulterers God will judge.

Hebrews 13:4

CONTENTS

Series Preface

Our mission with the *BIG TRUTH little books*™ series is to provide edifying, accessible literature for Christian readers from all walks of life. We understand that it is often difficult to find time to read good books. But we also understand that reading is a valuable means of spiritual growth. The answer? Get some really big truth into some little books. Every book in this series is only 5″ x 8″ and around 120 pages. But each is full of Scripture, theological reflection, and pastoral insight. Our hope is that Christians young and old will benefit from these books as they grow in their knowledge of Christ through his Word.

Cliff McManis, General Editor
Derek Brown, Series Editor

INTRODUCTION

On June 26, 2015, in *Obergefell v. Hodges* the Supreme Court of the United States (SCOTUS) took it upon themselves, in an unprecedented manner, to redefine God's sacred institution of holy matrimony. Before the decision was formally rendered, many knew ahead of time what the outcome would be based on the political makeup of the nine justices—four were liberal, four conservative, and the wild card was Justice Anthony Kennedy—a member of the Supreme Court for the past twenty-eight years—whose vote would tip the balance. He had already gone public on several occasions espousing his pro-gay preferences. And sure enough, when it came to vote, the liberal judges got their way with a 5-4 vote, undoing six thousand years of the historical preservation of heterosexual marriage.

As a pastor and shepherd, I began to think and pray about how I was going to address this issue. What would God have me say to my flock? On Friday of that week, the decision was unveiled. It was a five-to-four decision in favor of same-sex marriage. And with this legal decision, the Supreme Court was now redefining marriage to no longer refer exclusively to the union of a man and a woman. Marriage could now refer to the union of people of the same biological sex.

The next day, I received an email from one of the members in my church asking, "What do we do now?" About two hours later, I got an open letter from Pastor John MacArthur addressed to all alumni of The Master's Seminary, my alma mater. The letter was an exhortation from MacArthur saying that this decision was historic and unprecedented, and that we needed pastors everywhere to speak from God's Word and clearly address this issue. Essentially, he was saying, "Pastors, you need to tend to your local flock." That letter sealed the deal for me. It was a confirmation from my former pastor, and I knew that it was something that I needed to do.

This book is about God's definition of marriage. There are two parts to this book. The first part, chapters 1-3, will consist mainly of a biblical, theological, and historical discussion of marriage. The second part, chapters 4-5, will deal with questions of personal application: What should Christians do now in light of this historic legal decision? How should we interact with believers and unbelievers who are celebrating this decision? What should we think about our personal political involvement over this issue? I believe the Bible addresses all of these questions. Almighty God has given us an answer to these issues in His Word, and we are going examine each of them carefully in light of Scripture. We now turn to chapter one to consider the various factors that led to this historic decision.

~1~

History in the Making

Since June 26, 2015, I've entertained many questions from Christians about the Supreme Court's decision on so-called gay marriage. Some questions were theological, some personal, some societal, and some political. Before addressing some of those specific questions here, it would be helpful to take a brief diagnostic quiz. Diagnostic questions serve to identify a problem, or expose and manifest strengths and weaknesses that someone has on any given issue. Below are ten diagnostic questions related to this issue of gay "marriage." The purpose of this test is to prepare you for principles and arguments in this book on the issue of marriage while examining your thinking and exposing any misguided principles you may be harboring unknowingly. Hopefully this little test will help clarify some of the issues in your own mind. Each statement is either TRUE or FALSE. See how you do:

1. All federal and state laws in the United States are based on the majority vote of the people in our country.
2. A federal law that was established in 1857 that stated black individuals were considered "property," and not "people," was based on the majority vote of the American people.
3. A federal law established on January 22, 1973 that legalized abortion-on-demand was based on a majority vote of the American people.
4. The federal law that redefined marriage on June 26, 2015 was based on the majority vote of the American people.

5. Each nation of the world has the right to create its own definition of marriage.
6. The U. S. Supreme Court always makes the right and just decision when it renders a judgment.
7. Same-gender marriage is a social, political, and legal issue, and not a theological or biblical issue.
8. The Bible does not say anything about a definition of marriage.
9. The Bible does not address same-gender relationships.
10. The Church should let the state, government, and politicians dictate, manage, oversee, and even define the issue of what marriage is in our country today.

Let's grade the quiz. If you said FALSE for all 10 statements then you get 100%! I'll highlight a couple of these statements because they can be highly contentious and controversial, even among

Christians. The following section will be like Political Science 101 and, as you will see, what we learn here will become vitally important as we delve deeper into this discussion of gay "marriage."

FALSE: Laws in the U. S. are Based on the Majority Vote of the American People

How laws are established in America can be very confusing. Naively, a lot of Americans think that because the United States is a democracy it means we forge all of our laws by majority vote. We do not. Technically, the U. S. is a "representative republic" and not a pure "democracy." In fact, some of our nation's most significant laws are established by a process that is not dictated by a majority vote of the American people. The most obvious example is the election of President. In 1992, Bill Clinton became the President by receiving only 43% percent of the popular vote, which means the majority of American voters voted against him—57% of the people did not want him as President, yet he became President! That does not sound like "democracy." And again in 1996 Clinton became President again by receiving only 49% percent of the popular vote—meaning 51% voted against him, the majority did not want him, yet he was President a second term. In 1860, Abraham Lincoln received only 39% of the popular vote—the majority voted against him—and he still became President. Actually, eighteen times in U. S. history the man who became President did not garner a majority in the election.

So the preceding examples show that the majority does not necessarily rule in America. But at the same time, the majority does rule in some cases. When individual states put ballot measures up for a vote, many times all that is needed for a measure to pass is a majority vote. The same is true with city initiatives that come up for a vote on Election Day. So also when it comes to the Supreme Court of the United States (SCOTUS).

There are only nine judges, and when they render a ruling all they need is a majority—five votes—to interpret or establish law. And that is exactly what happened on June 26, 2015 when only five people determined what the definition of marriage would be for the other 320 million people who had no vote or say on the matter.

Prior to these five rogue Supreme Court Justices redefining marriage in 2015, at least 37 states had formally defined marriage as between one man and one woman through initiatives voted on by the people in those respective states. This means that virtually every time a vote was given to the people in a state to define marriage, the majority of the people voted for traditional marriage…not for gay marriage. This even proved to be true in liberal California with Proposition 8—the "California Marriage Protection Act," an initiative that defined marriage as one man and one woman.

Proposition 8 wasn't a divisive proposition. It

wasn't a statement of derision, prejudice, hatred, bigotry or exclusion, despite how it was spun by certain interest groups. The proposition simply read as follows: "Only marriage between a man and a woman is valid or recognized in California." This is what humanity has believed about marriage since time began. How controversial is that?

Opponents argued that Proposition 8 deprived people from same-gender relations, which is simply untrue. By way of reminder, same-gender relationships are not illegal in America, and they haven't been for many years. People have entered into same-gender relationships for years without government interference. Whether or not people could engage in such relations was never the issue. The issue was about *defining marriage*, and we cannot lose focus of that as we work our way through these vital issues.

Proposition 8 came to a vote in 2008 and

more than thirteen million Californians took to the ballot boxes. Atheists voted, Christians voted, Catholics voted, Mormons voted, Muslim Americans voted, Hindu Americans voted, secular Americans voted, Democratic Californians voted, and so on. There was a wide demographic represented in the people who voted for Proposition 8. The result? Over seven million people in California said, "Yes, I agree that marriage is between one man and one woman." About six million people voted against it. The people of California settled the matter Constitutionally.

As a result of the vote, the measure technically became part of the state constitution stating officially that the majority of the people of California believed marriage could only exist between one man and one woman. So, in 2008, according to the state of California, the decision that marriage was indeed between one man and one woman was determined by a majority vote of the people.

Despite the Constitutional vote of the people in California who affirmed Prop 8 by a large number, the will of the people has been sabotaged by five black-robed judges of the Supreme Court. This is where things get sticky. The Constitution of the United States is not a very long document, and I highly recommend that every American citizen read it. But you will read it in vain to find anything at all about the definition of marriage. This is a vital point because Supreme Court judges have one job—they are supposed to look at the Constitution to render a decision based on what is clearly delineated in the Constitution. They are supposed to make rulings only about what the Constitution says. They are supposed to interpret stated law, not make up law. Neither the definition of marriage nor the topic of marriage is mentioned in the Constitution. Therefore, the Supreme

Court has no jurisdiction on that topic.

If the issue at hand is not in the Constitution, the Supreme Court justices have no say and absolutely no business dealing with that issue. They are supposed to defer that matter to the states as stated in the Tenth Amendment of the Bill of Rights. Anything not in the Constitution is given to each of the fifty states to deal with themselves within their own government and among the state's residents. When this issue first came up and it was brought to a federal level, over thirty states in America were dealing with it themselves independently according to the Tenth Amendment, and California was one of them. This was entirely appropriate and fulfilled the function of the Tenth Amendment.

It is also important to note that thirty-four states put a definition of marriage on the ballot over the course of the past ten years, and thirty-four times in a row the people of those states voted in favor of traditional marriage. This fact goes to show that in every vote the majority of the American people believe in traditional marriage by definition. And that is the issue.

Back to Prop 8 in California. Over seven million Californian citizens voted legally and said, "This is what we believe a definition of marriage entails: one man and one woman." Seven years later over in Washington, D. C., five judges overruled the decision of seven million people living in California. That's what happened on Friday, June 26, 2015. That is tyranny and a clear abuse of power. And it doesn't matter what the issue is. If seven million people in California vote one way legally on an issue that is not delineated in the Constitution, and five judges in Washington—who were never elected and have no accountability—arbitrarily decide that they are going to overrule the decision of seven million people, that is an abuse of the Constitution, plain and simple.

Chief Justice Roberts affirmed in his

dissenting opinion that the five lawyer-judges have no right to create law by re-defining marriage and thus undermine the will of the people.

> [T]his Court is not a legislature. Whether same-sex marriage is a good idea should be of no concern to us. Under the Constitution, judges have power to say what the law is, not what it should be. The people who ratified the Constitution authorized courts to exercise 'neither force nor will but merely judgment'."

Justice Roberts was correct. The U. S. Supreme Court had zero authority to re-define marriage.

Historic Supreme Court Decisions

The U. S. Supreme Court has rendered egregious rulings before. One of them occurred in 1857 in the *Dred Scott v. Sandford* case. Dred Scott was a black American, born as a slave in Virginia. As an adult he lived in a free state, and sought legal action to gain his freedom. In 1857 the United States Supreme Court voted, 7-2, against Scott, denying him his freedom because the seven white, black-robed judges determined he was not a "citizen" but mere "property," i.e., some white person's slave. As mere property, black people could be sold, traded, beaten, deprived, given no rights and could even be killed. So much for the wisdom and justice of the U. S. Supreme Court.

The decision of these justices at that time in America was not based on the majority vote of the people. There were actually more people in America at the time in favor of freeing blacks from slavery than those who opposed. Eventually that decision in 1857 was taken out of the hands of the seven Supreme Court justices and went to the people; not by way of vote, but by way of the Civil War (1861-1865) that slaughtered over 650,000 Americans. In the end, the Union prevailed, and in time the Dred Scott Decision would be reversed.

The carnage of human lives resulting from the Civil War is unimaginable—much in part to the prejudice of seven judges. The Judge of the universe had already rendered His judgment about blacks at the beginning of creation. God said that all humans, no matter their skin color, are made in His image (Gen 1:26; Gal 3:28) and are therefore precious and equal. The Bible teaches that all human life is sacred. From the beginning God decreed that human life was so valuable that for one human to unlawfully take the life of another human warrants the death penalty (see Gen 9:6). Every human being is sacred, whether they are a Christian or not, regardless of the color of their skin. One of the greatest prophets in the Bible, Moses, was married to a black woman; and God approved of that sacred union (Num 12:1).

The Dred Scott decision is not the only deplorable decision rendered by the Supreme Court. Another was on January 22, 1973 with *Roe v. Wade* when seven judges ruled that a baby in the womb was not a person, and as such the mother could terminate its life. Up to that point in history, America had protected the lives of unborn babies in the womb. All throughout history, generally speaking, humanity believed the life in the womb was fully human. The conventional definition up to the time of *Roe v. Wade*, even going back thousands of years, was that human life began *at conception.* In 1973, seven justices voted in favor of *Roe v. Wade* dictating that life in the womb should be redefined from "baby" to the impersonal "fetus," a mere glob of cells and protoplasm and no longer possessing legal status as a human and no protection of life under the law. Thus, children *in utero* could be killed without legal recourse and on demand.

The leading justice who wrote the majority opinion rendered a decree that had never previously appeared in the history of American legal findings; namely, that the life in the womb is not a person. It's frightening to think that just one finite, fallen person determined whimsically, in terms of his terminology, that the unborn are not “persons,” and, therefore, are not protected by the Equal Rights Clause of the Constitution.

Once again, God the Creator and Judge of the universe already ruled on this matter in writing thousands of years ago. The Bible says that which is in the womb is a person made in the image of God. John the Baptist was filled with the Holy Spirit from the time he was in his mother’s womb (Luke 1 and 2). In Psalm 51:5, David reflected on the origin of life through the inspiration of the Holy Spirit, and stated that he became a person at conception. That is, God started relating to him personally at the moment he was conceived. In the Hebrew, it is very specific and it refers to even the time that he was conceived. From the time of conception, David took on a human sin nature, which implies that God began to relate to him in a personal way.

And those of you who are mothers and fathers know that as you touch a pregnant mommy’s tummy, you can feel the kicking and the rustling that's going on inside—that this is a baby. You've even given him or her a name and you've already developed a relationship with your baby while that child is in the womb. You even sing to baby and pray for baby. That child in your womb is a human made in God's image. But in 1973, seven people decided to overrule God's Word and now we have legal sanction to butcher babies while they are yet in the womb. Tragically, since 1973 up until 2016, nearly 60 million babies have been slaughtered in America.

The above scenarios clearly illustrate that we cannot rely on the U. S. Supreme Court to determine truth. Finite, fallen, capricious human judges don't get to define reality for the rest of humanity. Five unelected political officials don't have the right to say blacks are mere "property," or that unborn babies are not human or that the way God defined marriage in the beginning no longer stands.

Our Source of Hope

That is an overview of the politics involved in our current situation. If you're incensed by the political system and how it works, then you need to wake up to reality. Do not change your expectations. The United States government, the Constitution, the politicians—they are not your savior. Jesus is your Savior. Do not put your trust in men, as Scripture teaches very clearly. "Do not trust in princes, in mortal man, in whom there is no salvation" (Ps 146:3). This is probably one of the most important lessons we need to keep in mind with respect to this issue, and we also need to understand what God has to say on a very practical and personal level. Why? Because we need to be able to respond properly to significant cultural issues like this one.

To my surprise, when this decision by the Supreme Court went public, many professing Christians came out vociferously in favor of it. I was baffled that professing Christians would be celebrating the re-defining of God's sacred institution of marriage. Should Christians be celebrating this decision? Clearly, according to the Bible, absolutely not.

Maybe some of the people in favor of the majority decision are indeed Christians, and, for whatever reason, they are confused; maybe they don't really understand the issue or they are conflating two separate concerns. That is one reason why I am writing this book: I want to communicate that this issue is about the *definition of marriage* and not anything else. In order to remain clear-headed about this recent Supreme Court decision, we must clearly define the issue. This is not about whether Christians love people who are different than us. We are called to love people who are different than us.

I would suspect that a lot of these Christians are declaring agreement with the *Obergefell* decision for various reasons: out of ignorance, naivety, spiritual rebellion, personal relationships, or intentional pressure from other friends. For example, they might have gay friends and they are basing their opinion on a subjective personal experience or relationship rather than on what God's Word teaches. It is also possible that some professing Christians who are vociferously touting gay marriage are not actually born again and are not led by the Holy Spirit, yielding to Scripture.

Regardless of who you are or where you come from, you are engaging people on a daily basis. Maybe there are people in your family that are celebrating this Supreme Court decision—relatives that you have to deal with closely on a regular basis. How do you interact with them? As Christians—as God's witnesses—we need to have an answer and we need to have the proper mindset. We need to speak the truth in love (Eph 4:15). With that, let's look at the big picture overview before moving on to some practical application.

~2~

Marriage Belongs to God

Here in America, marriage has always been defined as the union of one man and one woman. America did not create that definition, nor did any country or individual craft that definition. Secular anthropologists and sociologists attempt to explain the phenomenon of marriage by arguing that it is an artificial social convention or construct that has developed over time. In other words, marriage is merely a byproduct of evolution. Specifically, they would argue that 25,000 years ago there was no marriage, but at some point, through evolution and the development of societal convention and norms, this institution called "marriage" was established and fine-tuned until it finally became monogamous between one man and one woman.

Secular sociologists also argue that because we are all going through the process of evolution, God has nothing to do with the morality of marriage. As a result, the definition of marriage should change, will change, and needs to change—or so says that great anthropologist, sociologist, philosopher and theologian, Whoopi Goldberg.

One weekday morning while driving my son to school I was listening to Whoopi's radio show. It was around the time that Proposition 8 was up for a vote in California. Whoopi emphatically told her listening audience that they need to reject Proposition 8, that marriage is not between one man and one woman, and that *the greatest need for the good of America and humanity is the abolition of the institution of traditional marriage altogether.* She described marriage as nothing more than a changing, evolving, artificial convention of a few elite people from time to time and culture to culture. She left God totally out of the equation.

Is that really how marriage came to be? Is it merely an artificial social convention and the byproduct of evolution? Is marriage essentially a western, white, Republican, Christian thing that we invented? Scripture is clear. The answer is, no. So, let's look directly at what the Bible has to say about this issue.

God Created Marriage

Where did marriage come from? The answer is simple: God created marriage. This truth is basic, but it is something we cannot afford to overlook or take for granted. Genesis 1 and 2 teach that God created everything out of nothing in six literal days. The Hebrew text is clear: this is not figurative language. The grammar, syntax, and the time references in the text indicate that Moses is referring to actual, historical events.

Throughout the Genesis narrative, Moses repeats the phrase "and it was so" after a series of creative events (see Gen 1:7, 9, 11, 15, 24). The phrase "and it was so" means "it really happened that way." Moses also repeats the phrase "And there was evening, and there was morning," at the end of each creation day (see Gen 1:5, 8, 13, 19, 23, 31). By way of emphasis, Moses was telling his readers that these were real days.

On the sixth day, at the culmination of creation, God declared that it was time to create humankind: God said, "Let Us make man in Our image, according to Our likeness" (Gen 1:26). Why the plural pronouns? God is talking amongst Himself. We learn from New Testament revelation that this is the Trinity: the Father, the Son, and the Holy Spirit (see Matt 28:19). God had chosen to make humans as persons: social, moral, religious, spiritual beings. That is what is involved in being created in God's image.

Verse 27 goes on to say, "God created man in His own image." How did God create man in His own image? The text explains: "In the image of God He created him; male and female He created them."

We learn from this Genesis narrative that one man and one woman together fully reflect the image of God by virtue of the attributes He has given us. That is the general reference to how God created humanity—one man and one woman. Then He instituted and created marriage. We can see how God specifically created the first two people and how He created the first wedding and the institution of marriage itself in Genesis 2:18-24:

> Then the LORD God said, "It is not good for the man to be alone; I will make him a helper suitable for him. Out of the ground the LORD God formed every beast of the field and every bird of the sky, and brought *them* to the man to see what he would call them; and whatever the man called a living creature, that was its name. The man gave names to all the cattle, and to the birds of the sky, and to every beast of the field, but for

> Adam there was not found a helper suitable for him. So the LORD God caused a deep sleep to fall upon the man, and he slept; then He took one of his ribs and closed up the flesh at that place. The LORD God fashioned into a woman the rib which He had taken from the man, and brought her to the man. The man said,
>
> "This is now bone of my bones,
> and flesh of my flesh;
> she shall be called Woman,
> because she was taken out of
> Man."
>
> For this reason a man shall leave his father and his mother, and be joined to his wife; and they shall become one flesh. And the man and his wife were both naked and were not ashamed.

Adam was by himself. But it wasn't good for him to be alone because God never intended to just have one man. Why? Among other reasons, because he could not perpetuate the race by himself. When Adam died, nobody would be left!

God intended to make the perfect

complement to Adam the man, and that's exactly what happened. Adam fell asleep and God literally took one of his ribs, closed up the flesh in that place, and with that rib fashioned the first woman (Gen 2:21-22). Does that sound impossible? Humanly speaking, it is impossible. Well, God does the impossible; He does miracles. He's God. Then God woke Adam to bring this beautiful, flawless, sinless first woman to him, and Adam's response is one of delight: "This is now bone of my bone and flesh of my flesh. She shall be called woman because she was taken out of Man" (Gen 2:23). God created and officiated the very first wedding. And the first wedding was between one man and one woman.

The first chapter of Genesis establishes one of the fundamental reasons God created marriage—to propagate the human race. In the beginning God told Adam and Eve to "be fruitful and multiply"—have babies (see Gen 1:28)! To do so would bring the blessing of God (Ps 127:3-

5). To avoid it and discourage it would bring God's wrath and displeasure (Gen 11:1ff). Only traditional, heterosexual unions can fulfill this basic purpose of human relationships. Same-sex sexual activity can't propagate the human race.

A comment needs to be made on the significance of the statement in Genesis 1:27 which says, "male and female He created them." God made it clear in the beginning that there are only two genders—male and female. Today in our warped culture, many are insisting there are actually anywhere from six to fifty-one different genders! Not so—just male and female. And one's gender is determined at conception and remains permanent until death. This is so because DNA determines gender, not how one "feels" or how one later "identifies" when one becomes a hormonally imbalanced, confused teenager.

Not even external body parts and genitalia determine gender; DNA in a person's cell does. Each person is conceived either as XX being female or XY being male. Based on the allocated chromosome makeup at conception, reproductive organs and systems are later added in accord with the DNA. No amount of hormone pills or external surgeries reconstituting body parts will ever change any person's DNA in every cell of their body, which will always be either XX or XY. God's design can't be altered by humanity's futile superficial experiments and ploys. From God's point of view, a transsexual person is still the same person they were when God gave them the breath of life at conception and will be judged before His throne as that person.

God Defines Marriage

The origin of marriage is found in God and described in Scripture. From God's perspective, marriage is foundational to the human race, for He created it before He created Israel and the Church. After He created marriage, God defined marriage in Genesis 2:24, which says, "For this reason a man shall leave his father and his mother, and be joined to his wife; and they shall become one flesh." The phrase "for this reason" establishes the perpetual reality for God's pattern for marriage—a divine, immutable formula that is the precedent for all history. God's pattern of one man and one woman is the precedent that will be binding for all humanity. Heterosexual marriage has been God's design from the beginning.

This passage is repeated several times in the New Testament (see Matt 19:4-6; Mark 10:1-8; 1 Cor 6:16; Eph 5:31) indicating that what was instituted and defined in Genesis is still the way God intends it to be. About 4,000 years after the first marriage, Jesus specifically taught on this passage from Genesis, declaring that the definition of marriage involves one man and one woman for life. Marriage was the mandate given to the Church as well, quoted by the apostle Paul (see Eph 5:22-33). In other words, in God's eyes, marriage hasn't changed. It's been the same for 6,000 years. Try as we might, man cannot usurp, undermine, or change the definition of marriage God established in Genesis.

Genesis 2:24 also teaches monogamous marriage—a singular man with a singular woman. This rules out any form of bigamy or polygamy. The verse says "a man" shall be joined to "his wife"—that is one plus one, which equals two…and no more than two. Adultery, the intrusion of a third party, violates this mandate. That's why God condemned adultery in the Old Testament as worthy of the death penalty (Lev 20:10). Also, the preservation of monogamy is the motive behind the seventh of the Ten Commandments (Exod 20:14).

The man is to cleave to his wife so that they might come together as a married couple and become a new entity. They become socially independent from all their family, and they become "one flesh." That is God's decree, and that is what He desires. A marital union between one man and one woman is blessed by God as

Genesis 2:25 goes on to explain: "And the man and his wife were both naked and they were not ashamed." There is complete sexual liberty and physical enjoyment in a marriage that follows God's design. That is the way it should be in a marriage relationship as it is blessed by God. God defined what marriage is. He said it is one man and one woman together before God as a covenant for life.

Heterosexual, monogamous marriage is affirmed and taught in the New Testament just as it was laid out in the Old Testament. The apostle Paul said that "each man is to have his own wife, and each woman is to have her own husband" (1 Cor 7:2). Paul also elaborated on the meaning of Genesis 2:24 when he wrote the book of Ephesians, particularly chapter 5:22-33.

In that passage, Paul actually quotes Genesis 2 in Ephesians 5:31. Paul's purpose is to explain God-ordained marital roles of man and wife in marriage. Men are to love their wives; wives are to honor and submit. And Christ and His Church are the example to follow. Men and women were equally made in God's image, yet have differing, complementary functions. And this is all in keeping with what God laid down in 4,000 BC between Adam and Eve, which is described in Genesis 2:24. God's design and definition of marriage is the same for all ages.

After Paul explains the basic definition and roles in human marriage in Ephesians 5, he concludes his discussion by revealing the greater eternal perspective about marriage in 5:32 when he says, "This mystery is great; but I am speaking with reference to Christ and the church." Here Paul speaks of a "mystery"—divine revelation that God gave him to reveal to others. This was new, or fuller information from heaven on the topic of marriage. The mystery of human marriage is that it is a finite, temporal picture of a coming eternal spiritual marriage between Christ and the glorified Church. The Church is Jesus'

Bride and He is preparing His Bride for a future heavenly wedding. John the Apostle describes this future heavenly wedding in the Book of Revelation:

> Let us rejoice and be glad and give glory to Him, for the marriage of the Lamb has come and His bride has made herself ready....Blessed are those who are invited to the marriage supper of the Lamb (19:7, 9).

The Supreme Court justices were not just tampering with a human institution when they distorted God's definition of marriage in June, 2015; they were actually skewing the ultimate heavenly reality of Christ's eternal betrothal to His Bride the Church, which is modeled in the living metaphor of earthly heterosexual, monogamous marriage.

If you are a Christian, you will be there at this final, divine, royal wedding as a participant because you will be part of Christ's Bride, the corporate Church. It is going to be a beautiful and glorious event. It is going to be a perfect wedding. And no misguided human authorities are going to thwart or sidetrack God's plans on the matter.

If you're a believer, you're going to be married eternally to Jesus Christ, and Paul says in Ephesians 5:22-33 that that is one of the main purposes for the institution of marriage. One man and one woman before God for life is an earthly picture of the spiritual reality of Christ married to His Church for all eternity. If you undermine the basic definition of marriage here in this life, then you distort the ultimate picture God has intended in the definition of marriage with Christ to His Church. That's probably one of the greatest ramifications of sin in this case. God created marriage, and He defined it. It is a picture of Christ and the Church.

God Defends Marriage

These are comforting truths. If you are a believer, and you have a biblical worldview, then you might have felt as though you had been punched in the gut on June 26th, 2015. Maybe you haven't even recovered yet. The greatest institution in all of humanity has been desecrated and undermined, from a human perspective. What do we do now? Well, *we don't panic*. God knows what happened. God knew it was going to happen. Marriage is His institution. He is in control of it; He is sovereign; He is all-powerful; He is all-knowing. He has a plan and it won't be overturned. Not only is marriage His creation, it's one of His most precious creations. That's sobering to think about, because God is a righteous God, a holy God, and a jealous God, according to Scripture (Ps 7:11; Lev. 19:2; Deut 4:24). God is jealous for that which is His own and that which is sacred to Himself. You don't tamper with marriage and get away with it. If you tamper with marriage, you are literally striking at the very heart of God Almighty. God defends marriage. He's been defending it for 6,000 years now, and He's not going to stop. He was not blindsided or surprised by what happened on June 26th.

Here are some high points throughout the Bible where God defends marriage:

- **Genesis 19** details the story of Sodom and Gomorrah. These were cities filled with sexual immorality, including rampant homosexuality and other practices that violated God's pure standard of heterosexual marriage. God warned Abraham that He was going to wipe out these two cities because of their corruption and immorality, and He did. That was an act of God protecting the sanctity of marriage.

- **Exodus 20** is where God gives the Ten Commandments. In the last six commandments that have to do with our relationship with other people, one of the commandants is, "Do not commit adultery" (Ex 20:14). The positive way of saying that is: "Be faithful to your spouse." The understanding here was that marriage entails one man and one woman for life. If you go outside of your relationship with your one spouse and commit adultery, you are violating the institution of marriage. That commandment was protecting God-given, heterosexual, monogamous marriage. God's penalty stated in the Mosaic Law for committing adultery was death by stoning (Deut 22:22; Lev 20:10). Not all sins warranted the death penalty, but adultery did. That is how severe it was, and that is how sacred marriage is to God.

- **Leviticus 18** has a list of sexual purity laws. With every one of them, the goal is to protect the sacredness of heterosexual, monogamous marriage. Many of those violations highlighted in Leviticus 18 warranted the death penalty.

- **Hebrews 13:4** is one of the clearest examples of this. It reads as follows: "Marriage *is to be held* in honor among all, and the *marriage* bed [*coitus*] is to be undefiled; for fornicators and adulterers God will judge." This verse has two clear commands followed by a warning. The two commands are that (1) all people need to honor the biblical institution of marriage as defined by God (whether you are a Christian or not), and (2) the act of sexual intimacy needs to be practiced only within the context of biblical marriage. Anyone who violates either of these commands is subject to God's wrath and judgment. When God created marriage in the beginning, He intended it as an institution for all humanity, not just for the Jews, or Christians. Marriage as God created it is to be "honored by all." If two Hindus want to get married, then it needs to be one man and one woman, for life. The same is true for two Mormons, Moonies or Muslims—one man and one woman—God is watching.

Dishonoring the Institution of Marriage

If we are called to honor the institution of marriage, it is important to know how we might potentially dishonor the institution of marriage. We dishonor marriage by abusing it, committing adultery, getting involved in immorality, ignoring marriage, or redefining it. There are many ways to dishonor it.

In the warning of Hebrews 13:4, the author of Hebrews gets very specific: "and the *marriage* bed is to be undefiled." In the New American Standard translation of the Bible, "marriage" is in italics because the word "marriage" is not in the Greek text. But a specific word, *coitus*, is in the text. *Coitus* is the act of sexual intercourse between a man and a woman. By definition, according to Webster's Dictionary, *coitus* refers to the "physical union of male and female genitalia." *Coitus* cannot happen between two people of the same gender—it's impossible. So, Hebrews 13:4 is one of the clearest texts demonstrating that sexual intimacy, as God designed it, is heterosexual and not some alternative. Hebrews 13:4 rules out homosexuality as a option when it comes to God's definition of marriage. The author of Hebrews is saying, "let *coitus* be undefiled," which means that sexual intercourse is to be enjoyed in the way God originally intended it, where husband and wife were brought together and they were naked and unashamed (see Gen 2:25).

Those are the only parameters and guidelines by which *coitus* should be practiced—between one man and one woman who are married for life. If you do it otherwise, you're violating it—whether you are single, whether you are a polygamist, or whether you're a heterosexual who sleeps with several partners who are not your spouse.

The sobering part is found at the end of Hebrews 13:4: "For fornicators"—those are people who engage in sexual immorality with total disregard for God's definition and standard of marriage—"and adulterers God will judge." That is a promise, and it is actually already happening. God has been judging fornicators and adulterers since Genesis 2. There *are* consequences for dishonoring marriage. Nobody is getting away with it. God is judging people whether they realize it or not (see Rom 1:18). God defends marriage.

Marriage Will Remain Intact as an Institution

It is important to uphold the truth that marriage is going to remain intact as an institution. It would be easy to think, given the way our culture is headed, that the institution of marriage as God has defined it is going to be obliterated or is simply on its way out. We know, however, that it will stay intact because it is God's precious institution. As we just observed, Revelation 19:6-9 shows that at the end of the age marriage is still intact with the greatest marriage of all—God to His Bride, the Church.

Likewise, in Matthew 24 Jesus explains that when He returns to the earth, He will find people "marrying and giving in marriage" (Matt 24:38). In other words, there are going to be people on earth doing what they have always been doing since the days of Moses: engaging in traditional marriage. At the time of Jesus' statements in Matthew 24, the only definition of marriage was the one provided in Genesis 2:24-25. We can have confidence, therefore, that even in the future, marriage will continue to be the norm around the world despite this temporary redefinition by the Supreme Court.

What Should We Expect?

Despite these clear biblical promises, believers need to remember that the sabotaging of traditional marriage is temporary from an *eternal* perspective. It could actually get worse immediately in our country and around the world for a while. If you think about the decision that was made with respect to abortion in 1973, we have not improved. We haven't overruled it; we haven't gotten rid of it. Babies—almost 60 million people—have died since *Roe v. Wade*. This ruling on marriage by the Supreme Court could be here in America to stay for quite a long time. Corollary nefarious consequences could come as a result of it and become law as well that are detrimental and totally undermine the Bible and your Christian faith. However, our encouragement and hope is found in that we know that God created marriage. He defined it and He will defend it.

~3~

WHY THE DEVIL HATES MARRIAGE

Satan Attacks Marriage

First Peter 5:8 says that the devil is your enemy and he prowls around like a roaring lion, seeking someone to devour. He wants to destroy and undermine anything with respect to God, Christ, the gospel, and biblical truth. Marriage is precious to God and so foundational to His plan, it has always been a major target of Satan all throughout history.

This is not the first time that marriage has been attacked or targeted. False religions have been doing this sort of thing for hundreds and thousands of years. We see this in Ephesians 6, where spiritual warfare is described in detail; believers are commanded to be on the alert and watch out for the devil, for he is on the prowl.

He is in the spiritual realm and he is attacking truth and believers constantly. Because of this, we need to put on our spiritual armor. This assault on marriage is not merely happening on a human level. This warfare is being fought on a satanic, supernatural, spiritual level.

Paul reminds us that "our struggle is not against flesh and blood, but against the rulers, against the powers, against the world forces of this darkness, against the spiritual forces of wickedness in the heavenly places" (Eph 6:12). As this battle is spiritual, our weapons need to be spiritual. Therefore, truth, prayer, and waiting on God and trusting in Him are our weapons. The weapons of spiritual warfare are not human weapons (2 Cor 10:4).

In 1 Timothy 4:1-5, the apostle Paul says that the Spirit explicitly told him that in latter times, some will fall away from the truth and from the Christian faith. "Some will fall away from the faith, paying attention to deceitful spirits and doctrines of demons by means of the hypocrisy of liars (4:1-2)." Anthony Kennedy, the Supreme Court justice who wrote the majority opinion on the ruling last summer, is a professing Roman Catholic. The position of the Roman Catholic is that marriage is between one man and one woman, and they're not budging on that. So even the Catholic Church has a proper biblical definition of marriage, and this judge is defying his own religion in these latter times.

This judge was deceived by his own sin, the lies of the world, deceitful spirits, and doctrines of demons. In the last days, there's going to be demonic doctrines or teachings and ideologies proliferating where we live "by means of the hypocrisy of liars." Those who undermine the institution of marriage are liars; they're hypocritical; their consciences are seared, according to Scripture. They don't listen to truth.

What are these demonic doctrines that are being propagated? We are told in the next sentence: "men who forbid marriage" (1 Tim 4:3). People are going to tamper with the institution of marriage, regardless of what it looks like—whether it be forced abstinence, polygamy, or a wholesale redefinition of marriage. Satan and his demons are continually going to attack the institution of marriage because it is so basic and so precious to God and His plan. Virtually every false religion and every false philosophy has a distorted or perverted view of sexuality.

Well, what do we do? We can start in the book of 2 Timothy 2:23-26, where Paul tells believers what they should *not* do. This should be our initial response until we keep praying and get God's leading and wisdom. 2 Timothy 2:23 says: "But refuse foolish and ignorant speculations." In other words, don't wrangle with people about this issue and get dragged into a dogfight that is totally unedifying. That's not going to accomplish anything. All it will do is produce quarrels.

Paul continues, "The Lord's bond-servant must not be quarrelsome" (2 Tim 2:24a). Paul is talking to Timothy as a pastor, but these instructions apply to every Christian because we are all servants of the Lord. Paul tells you to avoid arguing with your grandma, your aunt, your uncle, or your colleague at work about this issue. You can talk and dialogue and be civil, but if it goes beyond that, the conversation is over. You cannot be argumentative about it, "but be kind to all" (v.24b)—even people *in favor of this decree by the United States Supreme Court.* You need to be able to teach (v. 24c) and show people from the Scripture what God says. But you need to be patient and gentle with these people (v. 24d-25).

One believer told me, related to this issue of gay marriage, "I don't even know how to respond, because if I put anything on social media in opposition, I'm automatically stigmatized as a 'hater' or 'homophobic.'" That's true. Conversation has been so carefully nuanced and orchestrated, that if you respond negatively *at all*, you are immediately labeled a homophobe, a hater, a bigot, or simply unloving. It's almost like you can't even say *anything*. You've been pushed into the corner with a muzzle over your mouth. You can't even say just the positive things about traditional marriage because that is now perceived as being "narrow-minded."

Nevertheless, we need to respond in gentleness while speaking the truth in love (Eph 4:15). We can't be muzzled; we have to speak up. Paul isn't telling believers to fold or to be a doormat and appease everybody. But we must be careful not to respond and react emotionally. We must think it through, pray diligently over it, and search the Scriptures. Our conversations will be case-by-case, depending upon the person to whom we are talking. Having a spontaneous conversation with somebody on the street that you just met is very different than talking to a cousin who you will have to see for the next forty years at every holiday meal. When interacting with relatives on these tense and controversial issues it is always good to keep Ecclesiastes 3:7 in mind which says there's "a time to be silent and a time to speak," and keeping the balance is difficult.

There are also different contexts with which you'll be confronted where you will have the opportunity to speak up. So far, I'm allowed to speak clearly on this issue right now. I can talk and write very dogmatically as a minster of God. And we thank God for that freedom that we presently have. It's limited right now; we're in the minority. But isn't that the life of a Christian? In this present time, I have freedom. But who knows how long this freedom will last here in America? Thank God for all the shepherds in the pulpits around the world today doing this very thing—giving God's people God's truth on this issue. There is a voice. You're not going to hear this perspective from God's Word through secular mass media such as television, news websites or even radio. We're thankful for the treasure of His truth, the beauty of His Church, shepherds around the world, and Bible-believing saints who continue to boldly address this matter with a clarion voice.

~4~

WHAT NOW?

As believers, what do we do now? How can we practically apply this information into our daily lives? We've covered the basics of marriage starting in Genesis: that God designed marriage, God defined marriage, God defends marriage, and that Satan attacks marriage. Now is the time to follow that up with some practical applications. I will highlight six basic principles from God's Word to give you parameters by which to operate, to think, to live, to pray, to pursue, and also to be discerning as you encounter and engage this controversy in the trenches of daily living.

Others have come out publicly and spoken quite eloquently and authoritatively from

Scripture on this matter with great wisdom. I've been blessed by several of them. I think of my former pastor, John MacArthur, and his wonderful statement that I discussed earlier. Al Mohler, from Southern Seminary, has also written extensively on this issue with great wisdom that I know helped me personally. *Focus on the Family* actually had a very good summary statement on this from Jim Daly. Those things might help you and bless your soul. Anywhere that you can find helpful biblical resources on this issue, I encourage you to pursue them.

The first three points have to do with having a right perspective about our God, which really needs to be the foundation for practical living and where we go from there. The last three have to do with how Christians can implement some of these principles. I'm going to be taking you through a lot of Scripture in these next few pages. It's very important to actually look at God's Word as we work through the principles, so as you are able, look up the passages I reference in the following discussion.

Theological Principle #1: God is in Control

The truth that God is in control cannot be stated enough. Again, it is not a superfluous platitude; it is a reality. God's sovereignty is the theme of the Bible. God is in control.

Psalm 115

This is evident in Psalm 115, where we are given a couple of very specific phrases about God's control over the created order. God knew how this recent Supreme Court decision was going to be rendered. God wasn't blindsided or surprised by it at all. Even though this decision redefines marriage and undermines God's very definition of it, it doesn't have God shaking His head in shock or dismay at all. He knows what to do; He's still on the throne. All things work together for good as God is basically dictating history, and Psalm

115 is an amazing reminder of that.

When you know the God of the universe personally through faith in Jesus Christ, these promises can be real for you and guide your thinking. Psalms 115:1 says, "Not to us, O LORD," or Yahweh, which is God's personal name. The writer here has a personal relationship with the Creator of the universe, so he can use God's personal name. He is the God who keeps His promises; the God who loves His people. "Not to us, O LORD, not to us, But to Your name give glory Because of Your lovingkindness, because of Your truth. Why should the nations say, 'Where, now, is their God?'" Where is that Christian God? We've done away with Him and His principles! Here is the reality in verse 3: "But our God is in the heavens; He does whatever He pleases."

Isn't that awesome? God is in the heavens; He reigns over everything; He sees over everything; He controls everything. He knows what's going on. There are no surprises. He reigns supreme. And not only that, He does whatever He pleases! That is the God that we serve. That is the God that we know through Jesus Christ. And that statement also includes Jesus Himself, because Jesus is God. Jesus is Yahweh. Jesus is in the heavens. Jesus does whatever He pleases in addition to the Father and the Holy Spirit. God is in control. Do not feel like you've been jolted and undone because of some decree that five people in Washington issue and tyrannically foist upon the people. God is aware and He is in control.

The Book of Daniel

Now go to Daniel 2. Talk about tumultuous times—we haven't seen anything compared to what it was like in the days of Daniel, or even things currently transpiring in other places in the world. We still enjoy a lot of freedom here in America, but in the days of the Babylonian exile, Daniel, Shadrach, Meshach, and Abednego were slaves. They were forced into slavery, taken and kidnapped from their own country and forced to live in a pagan land under a brutal pagan King Nebuchadnezzar, with ungodly laws foisted upon them. That is the story of Daniel.

This takes place in about 580 B.C. Daniel and his three friends are Jews who have been kidnapped, who are being watched and brainwashed—or at least the Babylonian leaders are trying to brainwash them at this point. And Nebuchadnezzar is leading this effort. But God uses Daniel, and this faithful young believer understands that, despite the fact that he's been ripped away from his family and his homeland and been subjected to the culture and literature of Babylon, he still trusts his Lord. He knows his God; he knows that God is in control. God uses Daniel and actually gives him, through His Holy Spirit, a prophecy that he would eventually write down. God would later use this prophesy to encourage His people.

Here is what Daniel said regarding God being in control despite the circumstances around him that were much worse than what we are contending with in our country:

> Then the mystery was revealed to Daniel in a night vision. Then Daniel blessed the God of heaven; Daniel said, "Let the name of God be blessed forever and ever, for wisdom and power belong to Him. It is He who changes the times and the epochs; He removes kings and establishes kings; He gives wisdom to wise men, and knowledge to men of understanding" (Dan 2:19-21)

These truths are key. Power belongs to God. The Supreme Court's power is both limited and delegated, because it is received from God Himself. They may have abused the authority given to them, but it was given to them by God nonetheless.

Daniel also acknowledges that wisdom and power belong to God. "It is He who changes the times and the epochs" (Dan 2:21). That statement means that God is the author of history. If you look throughout 6,000 years of human history, you see a lot of trends: ebbs and flows, high points and low points, dictators who enforce inhumane laws, times of blessing—and God is totally in control of all of it. He raises up leaders and He removes them. Those who are in power—our president, our Supreme Court Justices—are all in their place of authority by God's ordination. God is the one that delegates authority. That is what Daniel 2:21 means. It is God who changes the times and the epochs.

Perhaps you are a little older. You've already seen many changes occur in American society—some for good and some for evil. Your experience fits in well with this reality that Daniel acknowledges; namely, that it is not humans that are changing the times and the seasons and the epochs and the trends and the events that are occurring all around us. It is *God* who is in charge and behind the scenes allowing all these things to happen. People are still accountable for their decisions, but it is God who changes the periods of world history. We have been in a period of world history under the American society for 200 plus years—that is an epoch.

Note verse 21: "He removes kings and establishes kings." There it is. Where in the world did this Supreme Court Justice Kennedy come from who made this ungodly decision about how to define marriage? How did he come into power? Verse 21 says that *God* is the one who removes kings and establishes kings. God puts all people in authority, not just kings. This includes the people who are in charge of the government here in America. We don't have monarchs and kings, but we do have presidents and senators and those who are in authority at a local and federal level. A Supreme Court justice would be in that rank. God literally removes and establishes Supreme Court justices who make the laws.

One thing we can do as believers during this

time of confusion and the abuse of power is thank God. We can thank Him that He is in complete control and that nothing can thwart His plan despite the abuse of power that is so typical of fallen humans.

In Daniel 4:1, we are given details regarding the lives of Shadrach, Meshach, and Abednego. King Nebuchadnezzar was a brutal, evil, tyrannical thug of a tyrant who was the most powerful man on planet earth at the time of Daniel. He had a major ego and built a massive statue of himself that was ninety feet tall. So he probably spent lots of money and years and used countless slaves to build this massive idol that he eventually called people from all over the world to worship. In a public assembly to dedicate this massive statue, Nebuchadnezzar demanded that the people bow down to this massive idol.

Not only did Nebuchadnezzar call all people to worship this idol, but he also made a decree that all *must* worship or they would be executed by being thrown into a fiery furnace. But Shadrach, Meshach, and Abednego didn't bow down. They violated the law. And they paid the consequences when the police came and got them and tied them up and threw them in the fiery furnace. They should have been incinerated before they even hit the bottom of the furnace, but God preserved them. God graciously saved them through a supernatural act. But they thought they were going to their death. And they exclaimed as they were being thrown in, "We're going to obey our God and not the laws of man. If we have to die for it, so be it."

By the way, God chastened Nebuchadnezzar and brought him low, worked on his heart, and I believe that God actually saved Nebuchadnezzar. People forget that. That would be like saying God saved Stalin or Hitler. Nebuchadnezzar was worse. And at the end of his life he recognized the God of heaven in verse 34:

> But at the end of that period I,

> Nebuchadnezzar, raised my eyes toward heaven, and my reason returned to me, and I blessed the Most High and praised and honored Him who lives forever; For His dominion is an everlasting dominion, And His kingdom *endures* from generation to generation. And all the inhabitants of the earth are accounted as nothing, but He does according to His will in the host of heaven And *among* the inhabitants of earth; And no one can ward off His hand or say to Him, "What have you done?" (Dan 4:34-35)

Can you imagine Hitler or Stalin saying this about the true God? That's what happened to Nebuchadnezzar. Nebuchadnezzar, who earlier in this book repeatedly said, "I will, I will, I will,"—which was a manifestation of his pride and arrogance—now says he's been changed; he's been humbled. And now it's not "I will," it's "thy will be done." God does according to His will. God is in charge. "He does according to His will in the host of heaven And *among* the inhabitants of earth; and no one can ward off His hand or say to Him, 'What have you done.'" That is an awesome reality in which we can find much comfort.

Theological Principle #2: God Defines Right and Wrong

This is a fundamental truth, but we need to be reminded of it. What happened on June 26th, 2015 isn't the first time something like that has happened in American history. It's not the first time it's happened in world history. It's happened repeatedly. Examples of it abound in Scripture. But the fact of the matter is that we need to be reminded that God is the one who defines right and wrong. There are human laws and there are divine laws, and sometimes those laws conflict. And we know that the truth is in God's laws.

This is clear in Isaiah 5, where God describes His own nation—His covenant people that He rescued and established, that He saved and brought through the desert and the Red Sea. Israel was to be His people, His children, His precious ones, and the apple of His eye. But they had become, by this time, more of a wayward child in the days of Isaiah. And so sin abounded throughout the nation of northern and southern Israel, and God had to chasten His people. He gave this description of the society as a whole, which can easily be used to describe our American society. God begins to rebuke Israel in Isaiah 5:3: "And now, O inhabitants of Jerusalem and men of Judah, Judge between Me and My vineyard." In verse 8, God begins to pronounce woes on His own people as a nation and as a people in light of the culture and their sin. "Woe to those who add house to house and join field to field, until there is no more room" (Isa 5:8). They had become greedy and compromised their convictions. God warns His people: "Woe to those who rise early in the morning that they may pursue strong drink" (Isa 5:11). As He continues through these woes, God denounces Israel's reversal of moral absolutes: "Woe to those who call evil good, and good evil; who substitute darkness for light and light for darkness" (Isa 5:20).

There it is. That's what we've done in our culture today. And not just on this issue and the definition of marriage, but on countless issues where as a nation we've called something good that is actually evil. This happened in 1973 when our government made a law that you could abort your baby legally. People actually celebrated this decision and said that it was good! It is good to kill a baby inside the womb! That's what many in the world are telling us and still tell us to this day. That baby in the womb is a precious life, and the murder of that life is evil, plain and simple. We are now being told that same-gender marriage is good, but God's Word is clear. Gay "marriage" is not a good thing—it is evil.

Pharaoh's Murderous Decree

In the early chapters of Exodus we learn of a Pharaoh who didn't like the Israelites. "Now a new king arose over Egypt, who did not know Joseph" (Ex 1:8). A previous Pharaoh had known Joseph and had a personal connection with God's people, but this new Pharaoh didn't have a relationship with Israel and he was threatened by this growing nation. As a matter of fact, he despised Israel and made laws that reflected his hatred. He took away all their freedoms and all their property, and then imposed unjust laws on them and made them slaves.

That's how human history flows. Culture and societal laws and norms ebb and flow based on who the leader is. And we could say the same here in America. "Now some new nine members of the Supreme Court arose over America. Five of them did not know the Constitution." That's what could go on for us today in America.

So this new wicked Pharaoh is intimidated by the Jews, and he makes this new law to oppress them. "The Egyptians compelled the sons of Israel to labor rigorously" (Ex 1:13). The

Egyptians "compelled" the Israelites. How do you compel a people to do something? You make laws. You decree it; you mandate it; you force it. That's what this text means. Here's an abuse of power defying the truth of the Bible that says every human being is made in the image of God. Pharaoh compelled the sons of Israel to become slaves, and then he continued to compel by making unjust laws and even physical abuse. Pharaoh even made a decree that when young Hebrew boys were born, they were to be put to death by being thrown in the Nile River. This was an edict—a law of a higher power. It was not made by nine Supreme Court justices; it was made by a monarch. But it's the same thing. So, the establishment of unrighteous laws by a ruling power is nothing new.

Nebuchadnezzar's Religious Decree

Let's revisit the book of Daniel. We've just examined Daniel, but I want to return briefly to highlight a couple of verses there about

Nebuchadnezzar. Look at some of the laws that he actually decreed. In Daniel 3:4 Nebuchadnezzar builds the idol. "Then the herald loudly proclaimed. 'To you the command is given'" (Dan 3:4). The herald is employed by the king to announce a new law. This would be like the White House telling CNN to announce a new law to the citizens of the United States. "Here's what the Supreme Court has decreed!" That's what the herald is doing. The law he has announced is binding on all people. What's the law? "'You are to fall down and worship the golden image that Nebuchadnezzar the king has set up. But whoever does not fall down and worship shall immediately be cast into the midst of a furnace of blazing fire'" (Dan 3:5-6). It's a twofold law. You bow down and worship, and if you don't, you're thrown into the fiery furnace. Fall down and worship. And it says everybody did in verse 7.

Then some informants told Nebuchadnezzar

that there were three Jewish young men—Shadrach, Meshach, and Abednego—who refused to worship the idol, which sent Nebuchadnezzar into a rage. And they brought the three men before him and cast them into the fiery furnace. How did these faithful young men answer to their charges?

> Shadrach, Meshach and Abednego replied to the king, "O Nebuchadnezzar, we do not need to give you an answer concerning this matter. If it be *so*, our God whom we serve is able to deliver us from the furnace of blazing fire; and He will deliver us out of your hand, O king. But *even* if *He does* not, let it be known to you, O king, that we are not going to serve your gods or worship the golden image that you have set up." (Dan 3:16-18)

These men were courageous and committed to obeying the Lord, even to their death. This is a tremendous story of bravery in the face of persecution, but it is also an illustration of another unjust, wicked law.

Local Restriction of Apostolic Preaching

Finally, let's look at one more bad law, found in the New Testament in the book of Acts. The twelve apostles are going through Jerusalem and they're preaching in the name of Jesus, and soon there's animosity and enemies of Christ who don't like the message being preached about Jesus. And so those that had local power abused the authority that God delegated to them. And they started making illegitimate laws that were hostile to Christianity.

> But when they had ordered them to leave the Council, they *began* to confer with one another, saying, "What shall we do with these men? For the fact that a noteworthy miracle has taken place through them is apparent to all who live in Jerusalem, and we cannot deny it. But so that it will not spread any further among the people, let us warn them to speak no longer to any man in this name." And when they had summoned them, they commanded them not to speak or teach at all in the name of Jesus. (Act 4:15-18)

The Jewish leaders made this decree. That's a law. Speak no more to anyone in the name of Jesus. This was another bad law. But how did Peter and John respond? "But Peter and John answered and said to them, 'Whether it is right in the sight of God to give heed to you rather than to God, you be the judge, for we cannot speaking about what we have seen and heard'" (Acts 4:19-20). A similar situation happens again a chapter later.

Again, the authorities were chastising the apostles, saying: "We gave you strict orders not to continue teaching in this name and yet, you have filled Jerusalem with your teaching and intend to bring this man's blood upon us" (Acts 5:28). And Peter and the apostles' response was when there are two laws that conflict—God's law and a human law—we will obey God's law (Acts 5:29). And that needs to be our response and our attitude as Christians. We need to obey God's laws, and when human laws undermine God's laws we stay faithful to God's laws, even though there could be consequences.

The normal practice for us as Christians, we know from Romans 13:1-7, is to obey the law of the land. In order to be good citizens, we should stop at red lights, we should obey the speed limit, and we should pay our taxes. Jesus said there is a beautiful balance in which we need to "render to Caesar the things that are Caesar's and render to God the things that are God's" (Matt 22:21). The definition of marriage is God's, so we need to honor that despite what the culture says and despite how hostile people may get. Render unto God the things that are God's. God defines right and wrong.

Theological Principle #3: God Will Punish the Wicked

Scripture is clear. The New Testament says, "the wages of sin is death" (Rom 6:23). Death is the consequence. Ezekiel says the same thing: "Behold, all souls are Mine…the soul who sins will die" (Ezek 18:4). God is holy and He must punish sin. God will punish the wicked. People aren't going to get away from their sins and their undermining of God's good laws. Romans 1:18-32 provides a summary of this principle.

We may not see righteousness in this area in our lifetime, by the way. You may not see the abortion law undone in your lifetime. Nevertheless, God is in control and He will punish the wicked. But because the Supreme Court's decision on marriage is now a federal law, it affects our entire country; it's now the mindset of millions of people. And as a result, there are going to be massive cultural consequences. Romans one speaks directly to this. In Romans 1:18-32, God is speaking to sinful individuals who together make up a sinful culture. There are cultural implications in Romans 1:18-31, and you will see that there are many parallels in this passage to what's going on in America today and many other secular, ungodly countries.

For the wrath of God is revealed from heaven against all ungodliness and unrighteousness of men who suppress the truth in unrighteousness, because that which is known about God is evident within them; for God made it evident to them. For since the creation of the world His invisible attributes, His eternal power and divine nature, have been clearly seen, being understood through what has been made, so that they are without excuse. For even though they knew God, they did not honor Him as God or give thanks, but they became futile in their speculations, and their foolish heart was darkened. Professing to be wise, they became fools, and exchanged the glory of the incorruptible God for an image in the form of corruptible man and of birds and four-footed animals and crawling creatures. Therefore God gave them over in the lusts of their hearts to impurity, so that their bodies would be dishonored among them. For they exchanged the truth of God for a lie, and worshiped and served the creature rather than the Creator, who is blessed forever. Amen.
For this reason God gave them over to degrading passions; for their women exchanged the natural function for that which is unnatural, and in the same way

> also the men abandoned the natural function of the woman and burned in their desire toward one another, men with men committing indecent acts and receiving in their own persons the due penalty of their error. And just as they did not see fit to acknowledge God any longer, God gave them over to a depraved mind, to do those things which are not proper, being filled with all unrighteousness, wickedness, greed, evil; full of envy, murder, strife, deceit, malice; *they are* gossips, slanderers, haters of God, insolent, arrogant, boastful, inventors of evil, disobedient to parents, without understanding, untrustworthy, unloving, unmerciful; and although they know the ordinance of God, that those who practice such things are worthy of death, they not only do the same, but also give hearty approval to those who practice them. (Rom 1:18-32)

Note verse 18: God's wrath "is revealed"—present tense. Literally it says, "For the wrath of God is being revealed right now." That means the wrath of God is presently being poured out by God on all ungodliness and unrighteousness of men. This outpouring of wrath did not just begin on June 26th, 2015. This has been going on all throughout human history wherever there has been sin.

God pours out His wrath on sin in many different ways. One of the ways that God pours out His wrath in Romans 1:18-32 is by letting people do what they want. That's one of the forms of God's wrath—just letting go, taking away the restraints and letting people consume themselves with their sin. And that's what Paul says three times in this passage. God "gave them up."

And thus begins this spiral and cycle of sin downward into the gutter of an entire human race. That is the wrath of God that's being poured out on unrighteousness. This outpouring of wrath isn't in the form of lightning bolts coming out of heaven or earthquakes swallowing whole civilizations; rather, it is seen through God's providence and the choices of sinful man. I conclude that Romans 1:18-32 is an accurate description of America.

People know the truth because God has put it in them; it is in their conscience. People were made in God's image and they suppress, reject, and deny that truth. God created every human being in His image with both a conscience and a very real, immediate, and intuitive knowledge of His existence and identity as the Creator who is to be honored. Every person has that moral barometer from the time they're born. And that's what they're suppressing, rejecting, and denying.

Paul continues: "Because that which is known about God is evident within them" (v. 19). That's the conscience. So Richard Dawkins, for example, the most famous atheist in the world, is not really an atheist. He's deceived and deceiving others. He is a theist; he's suppressing the truth that he knows intuitively about God. And he's suppressing this truth because of his sin. That's what Romans is teaching—there are no real atheists. Why can we say this? "Because that which is known about God is evident within them; for God made it evident to them" (v. 19). Paul is arguing that by virtue of creation and being made in God's image, man knows that God exists. How has God made His existence known to all his human creatures? "For since the creation of the world His invisible attributes, His eternal power and divine nature, have been clearly seen, being understood through what has been made" (v. 20).

Paul is not saying that people know God personally, but only they know He is the Creator and that they are accountable to Him. People know He is the Judge, which is why people fear death. They must face the Judge and the Creator. But they refuse to give God His deserved glory. "They did not honor Him as God or give thanks, but they became futile in their speculations, and their foolish heart was darkened. Professing to be wise, they became fools, and exchanged the glory of the incorruptible God for an image in the form of corruptible man and of birds" (vv. 20-21). In other words, every human being is worshipping something. And if they're not worshipping the true God, they're going to worship something else, even if they call themselves atheists. They're going to worship something—whether it's money, power, themselves, or whatever—because we're all religious creatures by virtue of creation and being made in God's image.

But God exercises judgment against those who turn away from Him. "Therefore God gave them over" (v. 24a). That's God's wrath. He's going to give them over to the lusts of their hearts. One of the sins that characterize unbelievers is sexual immorality, and there comes a point where God removes the restraint from their passions. What happens? Mankind indulges in sexual sin, and their conscience becomes seared "so that their bodies would be dishonored among them" (v. 24b). Paul summarizes the reason for this judgment: "For they exchanged the truth of God for a lie, and worshipped and served the creature rather than the Creator, who is blessed forever" (v. 25).

Verse 26: "For this reason God gave them over to degrading passions." Now the sexual sin in which they indulge is getting worse. "For their women exchanged the natural function for that which is unnatural"—women engaging in sexual intimacy with other women (i.e., lesbianism). That's what this verse is talking about. And the same sin occurs among the men: "And in the same way also the men abandoned the natural function of the woman and burned in their desire toward one another, men with men committing indecent acts and receiving in their own persons the due penalty of their error" (v. 27). Men engaging in sexual acts with other men is not only a sin, but a sign of God's judgment and wrath.

And then, finally, verse 28: "And just as they did not see fit to acknowledge God any longer, God gave them over." That's the third time Paul says that God "gave them over." To what did God give them over? "God gave them over to a depraved mind" (v. 28b). The result of their depraved mind was to plunge themselves into all kinds of sin and, as Paul says, "to do those things which are not proper." Now mankind engages in the entire spectrum of possible rebellion against God and applauds those who join them in their sin. You can see this spiritual reality played out all across our country.

Understanding the spiritual condition of fallen mankind helps us to understand how some of the justices on the Supreme Court voted the way they did. Justice Kennedy has never said that he is homosexual, yet he gave hearty approval to it by the judgment he rendered. And that's what Romans said would happen. But the point of Paul's argument is that God will punish. No one can get away with sin.

So God is in control, God defines right and wrong, and God will punish the wicked. These are three essential theological principles we must keep in mind as we face our culture post-*Obergefell.* We now turn in chapter five to consider a few points of practical application.

~5~

KEEPING THE PROPER PERSPECTIVE

There are so many principles we could think through, but we've got to keep the proper balance, which is hard to do in difficult situations and topics like this one. Here are four simple principles to keep in mind:

Practical Application #1:
Speak the Truth in Love

There is an important passage in the book of Timothy that we've already examined that talks about not being quarrelsome (2 Tim 2:24). Scripture exhorts us to not quarrel with people about this issue; don't be argumentative in an unedifying, disrespectful way.

However, Scripture does not say that we

should be silent on issues like this one. Don't be silent; don't be a doormat; don't be muzzled. That's not God's calling for the Christian. God wants believers to be vocal for Him. We represent Him; we are the salt and the light of the world. We are to manifest truth on His behalf, and one of the main ways we do that is by speaking.

That's why Ephesians says to speak the truth and speak the truth in love (Eph 4:15). Jesus is the master model of how to blend truth and grace. Interestingly, however, many people believe the Gospels are nothing more than warm and cuddly stories, with Jesus holding children on His lap and walking in the cool weather with His disciples along the coast of the Sea of Galilee, always being nice and happy. But that's not what we find in the New Testament accounts of Jesus' life.

When I preached through the entire Gospel of John, one thing that stood out to me was that

Jesus seemed to get in a fight in almost every chapter! Most of those times He's arguing publicly with the Jewish authorities. And it culminates in chapter 8, when there's a public discourse going on and they're calling Jesus all kinds of names, and He calls them the "children of the devil" (John 8:44). This was a public statement—during a holiday in Jerusalem.

In Luke and Matthew you find the same scenario. Jesus is getting into it in every single chapter with the Pharisees! Jesus isn't always being "nice." What is He doing? He is speaking the truth and He is doing it in love. The hypocritical religious leaders are the ones becoming hostile, angry, divisive and eventually murderous. That's what happens when the truth is spoken clearly and forthrightly. Jesus said, "I did not come to bring peace, but a sword" (Matt 10:34). What did Jesus mean by this statement? Simply this: the truth will divide. That's what truth does. Some people just don't want to hear spiritual truth. It makes them mad. You can say it as gentle as you want and even use soft tones. But when the natural man hears the truth, he is enraged by it. That's what Jesus meant. Nevertheless, we are to speak the truth in love. So that's the balance. Speak the truth and do it in love with gentleness and reverence, in the words of Peter (see 1 Peter 3:15). But we can't be muzzled.

You might have to say that homosexuality is a sin. A lot of people are afraid to say that today. "That doesn't sound loving. I might be stigmatized! I might be called a homophobe! I might be ostracized! I might be thrown in jail!" It doesn't matter. The Bible is clear—Leviticus 18:22 and Leviticus 20:13 say that homosexual practice is sinful and wrong; it is an abomination in God's sight. That's what Scripture says.

The New Testament says the same thing. As a matter of fact, Paul is explicit in this regard in his first letter to the Corinthians.

> Or do you not know that the unrighteous will not inherit the kingdom of God? Do not be deceived; neither fornicators, nor idolaters, nor adulterers, nor effeminate, nor homosexuals, nor thieves, nor *the* covetous, nor drunkards, nor revilers, nor swindlers, will inherit the kingdom of God. Such were some of you; but you were washed, but you were sanctified, but you were justified in the name of the Lord Jesus Christ and in the Spirit of our God. (1 Cor 6:9-11)

"Do not be deceived." Paul is talking to Christians. Wake up! Don't be fooled by what you're hearing and what people are saying in society! Think like a Christian, not like the culture! In other words, think biblically. Do not be mislead by lies or by the father of lies, Satan himself! In what areas are Christians susceptible to deception? We are susceptible to being deceived about what kind of lifestyle corresponds with salvation. Paul explains that immoral people *will not* enter the kingdom of God. Neither will the effeminate, or the adulterer, or, as Paul states clearly, homosexuals enter the kingdom of God. It is likely that some will try to persuade you to think that it is possible to live in direct violation of Scripture yet receive salvation at the end of time. That is why Paul is telling the Corinthian church and the rest of us: don't be fooled at this point.

So we must speak the truth, speak it in love, and hold firm to what Scripture teaches, but balance that with staying focused on the fact that Jesus died for *all sin*. Yes, homosexuality is a sin, but that's why Jesus came to earth. That is the very reason that Jesus came. That's the good news! You have to give people the good news by saying, "You know what? You can be forgiven of that sin; you can be liberated from that sin; you can be set free from that sin. You can be adopted into God's family." That is precisely why Jesus came. He came into this world to be punished for *all sin*. He died on the cross for *every sin*—for lying and adultery and heterosexual sin and homosexual sin and theft and everything else.

That is the good news. Jesus died for your sin, and if you believe in His gospel and are willing to confess your sin and repent, He can save you and forgive you. Jesus didn't come into this world to those who are healthy. He came to those who were sick and needy as the Great Physician (Matt 9:12). His very purpose was to seek and to save those who were lost (Matt 18:11). We need to speak the truth and we've got to point out sin, but this needs to be balanced with the gracious good news. Any time we point out sin, it's really just laying the groundwork for the gospel and for the glorious good news of Jesus Christ. And then we can give them the promise of Isaiah 55:1: "Ho! Every one who thirsts, come to the waters; And you who have no money come, buy and eat. Come, buy wine and milk Without money and without cost" and Ezekiel 18:32: "Repent and you will live!" Isn't that great news? Repent and you will live. Turn and God will forgive all of your sin. I love this phraseology in Isaiah:

> Let the wicked forsake his way, and the unrighteous man his thoughts; and let him return to the LORD, and He will have compassion on him, And to our God, For He will abundantly pardon. (Isa 55:7)

Practical Application #2:
Keep the Right Priorities

What are the right priorities? Well, our priority is the gospel. It starts here, first. And the definition of marriage is a priority. But if you think you're going to argue a whole bunch of unbelievers into accepting your biblical view of marriage, that's futile thinking. Most of the truths in the Bible, if not all of them, I accept and believe because I'm a Christian and because I have the supernatural ability and capacity to believe as I'm empowered by the Holy Spirit. If you think you can argue with an unbeliever and get him or her to believe in the biblical doctrine of creation, for example, that's not going to happen. That's not even our job. The only reason I believe in hell is because it's in the Bible and because I have the Holy Spirit Who helps me believe. If I wasn't a Christian, I wouldn't believe in hell. How do I know that? Because when I wasn't a Christian, I didn't believe in hell. I only believed in hell *after* I became a Christian. So we've got to maintain the right priority. Keep the right priorities: the gospel and caring for the individual to whom you are talking.

Going along with keeping the right priorities, I have a list of a couple "don'ts". Don't argue with people needlessly. And don't boycott people over this issue. As Paul reminds us, we cannot boycott unbelievers because otherwise we would have to leave the world (1 Cor 5:10). "I'm not going to buy my Wonder Bread from that 7-Eleven because the owner at that 7-Eleven is an atheist!" Good luck finding a 7-Eleven, or any food market that is not in some way connected to things you don't believe in. You'll never get your

Wonder Bread!

A couple believers brought this issue of boycotting up to me because they were concerned as they were dialoguing with other Christians. They were pointing out that it seems like a lot of Christians they know were saying that homosexuality is the worst sin—the unpardonable sin—and that it's worse than all other sins. And these Christians were saying that we're supposed to boycott homosexuals, but they don't have a problem not boycotting other people and other sins. It shouldn't be that way. Homosexuals are just like any other sinners. So don't boycott, and also don't be a coward. Don't be like the arctic river, which is frozen over at the mouth. Do not be afraid to say something. Speak up for God.

Practical Application #3:
Maintain the Right Perspective

This earth is not our home. Heaven is our home, and we eagerly await for our Savior, the Lord

Jesus Christ, who will come in glory and save us and transform our lowly bodies into glorious resurrection bodies (Phil 3:10). Society is getting worse. If you think society is getting better, you need to change your thinking. The apostle Paul said through the Holy Spirit that times are waxing worse and worse and men themselves are going from bad to worse (2 Tim 3:13). We're not trying to save society—we can't.

Another thing to help our perspective is the reality that we are in the minority as Christians, and we need to get used to it. There is no moral majority, or Christian majority—not in America. "There will be few who find it," said Jesus (Matt 7:14). Narrow is the way; narrow is the gate.

Finally, we were called to suffer as Christians. Paul said that believers will endure persecution in this life. Philippians 1:29 says that you were called not only to believe in Christ, but also to suffer for His sake. So, you're being ostracized? You're being yelled at? You're being cursed? You're being persecuted? None of these things should be a surprise. As a matter of fact, Jesus said to count yourself blessed if people say evil and all manner of horrible things about you (Matt 5:11-12). Count yourself blessed, for you are on God's team. They did the same thing to your blessed Savior, the Lord Jesus Christ.

Titus 3:1-7 is also a wonderful passage that helps give us the proper perspective on this complicated, difficult, divisive issue: "Remind them to be subject to rulers"—the pagan rulers; the ungodly rulers in so far as their laws don't violate God's laws—"to authorities, to be obedient, to be ready for every good deed, to malign no one, to be peaceable, gentle, showing every consideration for all men" (vv. 1-2). Why? Because "we also once were foolish ourselves." Before we got saved, we were disobedient. We were deceived by our own sin and by Satan himself. We were "enslaved to various lusts and pleasures, spending our life in malice and envy, hateful, hating one another" (v. 3). But something incredible happened to us. "But when the kindness of God our Savior and His love for mankind appeared, He saved us, not on the basis of deeds which we have done in righteousness." We didn't do anything to save ourselves—it was all God and His grace. He saved us "according to His mercy, by the washing of regeneration and renewing by the Holy Spirit, whom He poured out upon us richly through Jesus Christ our Savior."

Practical Application #4:
Persevere in Prayer

James 5:16 says, "The effective prayer of a righteous man can accomplish much." Biblical prayer is powerful. God does miracles and changes hearts by responding to the prayers of the saints. The act of prayer is a response in faith—and acting in faith pleases God. With respect to a rogue government redefining God's definition of marriage, there is much to pray for.

Pray that God's will be done here on earth as it is in heaven (Matt 6). God's "will" is what God wants. God wants His institution to honored among all. Pray accordingly. Also, pray that God would protect His institution of marriage through righteous leaders and political officials. First Timothy 2 exhorts Christians to pray for the government rulers who in turn would rule in favor of civility. Plead with God to convict rulers to make the right decisions on holy matrimony and also that they would reverse bad decisions that undermine His honor. I'm reminded of Acts 12 when Peter was in prison for preaching Jesus. The Jerusalem saints prayed to God on his behalf, and God answered by setting him free. Prayer changes things!

CONCLUSION

Confusion about the definition of marriage is rampant in the world today. TV, the Internet, Hollywood, self-serving politicians, and the ubiquitous liberal news media all reinforce and propagate that confusion. Today we are told to believe "gay is OK" and even preferred over traditional marriage. We are also told to believe that being gay is normal and fulfilling. But the Bible is clear. To believe any of that is to be "deceived." That is what 1 Corinthians 6 says—Paul warned Christians in the secular, immoral, perverted culture of Corinth saying, "Do not be deceived….homosexuals will not enter the kingdom of God." That warning still stands.

This little book was written for Bible believing Christians, to remind them of basic truths regarding God's holy institution of marriage and why it is important to courageously defend it as a foundational ordinance for the general stability of human civilization. This is not overstating the case. I trust you picked up on the main principles of this truth as you read.

Instability was forced upon us with the egregious ruling of five unelected judges, on June 26, 2015, when they arbitrarily proclaimed that marriage is no longer to be defined as a union between one man and one woman—marriage is to be understood as same gender as well. We highlighted that the U. S. Supreme Court does not trump God's Word. The Supreme Court has rendered horrific rulings before, like in 1857 when they said that black Americans were not "people" but just "property" with no rights. And their ruling in 1973 when they ruled that babies in the womb were not people but just globs of protoplasm, also deserving no rights or protection under the Constitution.

These rulings are not just secular and pagan; they are truly barbaric and heinous. God will not be mocked (Gal 6:7). Vengeance is His (Rom 12:19). He hears the countless voices of the innocents whose spilt blood ceaselessly cries out from the ground pleading for vengeance (Gen 4:10; Rev 6:10). In His time, it will come (2 Thess 1:5-10).

Marriage belongs to God. He created it in the first week of human history as taught in the book of Genesis. God defined marriage as being between one man and one woman for life who become one flesh in a sacred covenant. One basic purpose of marriage is the procreation of the race. Same-gender relations subvert that divine plan. God also defined marriage, establishing the roles of husband and wife as well as instituting penalties for the violation of the marriage covenant.

We also saw that God is committed to defending marriage with a vengeance. Hebrews

13:4 and 1 Thessalonians 4:3-8 and many other passages give warning to those who would trample on God's model and plan for marriage. He is committed to protecting the ultimate reality of marriage—the future coming wedding of Jesus the groom to His precious Bride, the Church. God is sovereign and all-powerful. As such, His institution shall remain intact continuing on in perpetuity.

Scripture reminds us that the ceaseless assaults against marriage and sexual purity are rooted in Satan's evil antics behind the scenes in the spiritual realm. Satan is real. But God has given us the needed spiritual tools to counter him in warfare—the truth of His Word, faith and prayer. This is God's sufficiency for us.

This battle will continue as long as we live in this fallen, cursed world. In the meantime, we as believers walk by faith not by sight, knowing that complete redemption and glory is our future inheritance. Perfect justice is coming with the second return of the Lord Jesus Christ in glory. The wait is worth it. Until then, we lean upon His grace, fight on, all the while praying, "Maranatha! Come Lord Jesus!"

ABOUT THE AUTHOR

Rev. Cliff McManis has been in pastoral ministry since 1989. He graduated from The Master's College with a B.A. in Biblical Studies and earned an M.Div. from The Master's Seminary. He went on to earn his Th.M. and his Ph.D. in Ecclesiology from the Bible Seminary in Independence, Missouri. He is the author of several books including *Christian Living Beyond Belief, Biblical Apologetics, What the Bible Says About Gray Areas, What the Bible Says About Government* and editor and contributing author of *Rescued by Grace.* He has served in churches in southern California, Utah, Texas, and the San Francisco Bay Area, and has been the teaching pastor of Grace Bible Fellowship since its inception in 2006. He and his family currently reside in Cupertino, California.

Made in the USA
San Bernardino, CA
24 July 2017